T0195075

DO YOU WANT TO GO TO COLLEGE NOW?

HULDAH OHENE KENA

authorHOUSE®

AuthorHouse™
1663 Liberty Drive
Bloomington, IN 47403
www.authorhouse.com
Phone: 833-262-8899

Published by AuthorHouse 08/07/2021

ISBN: 978-1-6655-1769-0 (sc)
ISBN: 978-1-6655-1768-3 (e)

Library of Congress Control Number: 2021903578

Print information available on the last page.

CONTENTS

Dedicated to those hungry for a better tomorrow

INTRODUCTION

My name is Huldah Ohene Kena. You might be wondering what compels a college graduate to write a book about going to college. Well, I will tell you that I feel a responsibility to all immigrants, first-time college students, and people who simply want a chance at a higher education like me. My experience as a college student has been a series of ups and downs. However, I was able to accomplish my degree in science. If someone had told me half of the things I am about to share with you, I think I would have spent less money, gained more opportunities, and been a better student in undergrad.

My simple mission is to be a guide to those who seek knowledge and want a better tomorrow for themselves. I hope that all people, regardless of their race, gender, or skin color, receive this knowledge and achieve their dreams, despite all challenges and odds that stand in their way. Remember that everything is simply a process and can be achieved with the proper guidance. You can and will achieve your goal, and I promise to help each and every one of you through the process. Let us begin!

CHAPTER 1

COMING TO AMERICA

Time does fly. It feels like yesterday that I came off the Alitalia flight at JFK airport. December 2020 marked sixteen years since I became an immigrant in the United States. It was a very cold day in December 2004, and my mother and I were both exhausted from the flight from Ghana. When we finally arrived at the Pittsburgh International Airport, we were greeted with the coldest breeze of the winter that year. I remember feeling so numb and outnumbered.

There were no kids on the airplanes, only adults. Most of them looked so busy, and they made me nervous. I remember calling my dad at different points throughout the journey to ask for directions or simply to hear his voice. It was at JFK airport that I noticed the different kinds of faces that were not like mine. I had no idea so many different kinds of people existed. Back in my home country, there were only brown people. Once in a while you would see a white person, but they were usually tourists, doctors, or people who worked at the Ghanaian embassy.

I must admit, when we arrived at the Pittsburgh airport, I was happy because my family was together for the first time in a long time. I don't remember much about the ride to the apartment my dad lived in because I slept through the whole drive. But I do remember seeing so much snow and feeling cold. I was so disappointed when we arrived at a little house beside other little houses. For some reason, I had expected something bigger, nicer, more like the houses I had seen in the movies my dad had brought to Ghana on visits.

The only thing I looked forward to was going to school. I stayed home for about two weeks and then asked my parents when I could start school. I was enrolled in the local middle school in my neighborhood the next day.

Just like me, most of you are coming to America to get access to a better education. You might not be coming as kids like I did. Perhaps you are teenagers or adults. No matter what age you are, if you have a will, there's a way. As an immigrant going to school, the first thing you must know is that America is a country filled with immigrants.

Although you might feel alone and outnumbered at times, you might also feel like the center of attention, in the worst way. Keep in mind that your classmates, parents, or grandparents went through what you are going through now. I also learned it was hard to fit in. Kids might make fun of you for the way you pronounce words or wear your hair or the kind of clothes you wear to school. In America, those things are important for some reason. Your appearance will determine how quickly kids warm up to you as an immigrant from a different country.

In my experience, students who come from rich backgrounds or developed first-world countries assimilate better. Sometimes students who look like Americans or immigrants who have already blended into the melting pot of American culture also assimilate faster. Children who come to the US from countries that do not speak English as a first language have to take a special class or classes for some time away from the rest of their classmates. You might have to take a class called English as a second language, or ESL. All students, young or old, have to take this class. Most ESL teachers are well-rounded and have met people and children from all countries, cultures, and languages. Your ESL teacher will be your guide and even your new best friend.

If English is a second language for you and you only know a few words, you will need more time as an ESL student. However, if you are well acquainted with the English language, you might be an ESL student for a short period. To pass the ESL class, you need to take the English proficiency exam. After this, you will probably take the general educational development test, or GED, if you are an adult. Children will either attend middle school or high school. Most of the people you will get close to will be your teachers, classmates, and, yes, you have *me*.

A couple of things to keep in mind: Don't be afraid to stand up for yourself. Remember who you are because your classmates, and even your teachers, will try you. They will want to know the kind of person you are and will try to put labels on you. They will want to put you under their umbrella of stereotypes that might be untrue. A few of the most common stereotypes I faced as a Ghanaian immigrant were that I was poor, lived in a jungle or a hut, and had never worn shoes before. They thought I could run like a gazelle or had a pet monkey or that my father was a lion tamer and my mother wore a grass skirt. They even believed I would be in an arranged marriage.

As horrendous as these stereotypes might be, those were things students and other people told me. Whatever people have seen on television about your country creates stereotypes. Sometimes it is very hurtful to hear. People want to believe in their preconceived notions. You should let them because with time they will get to know the real you and they will love you. No matter what, everyone might not like you or be on your side, but I promise you that you will find the right people who appreciate you for simply being you. Know that you are enough. I promise that's half the battle.

CHAPTER 2

GED OR HIGH SCHOOL

Depending on your level of education, the very first step to get ready for your future goal is to obtain a high school diploma or a GED. It helps adults get their high school education. GED classes are offered by a lot of companies as well as by community colleges. Some programs allow students to earn college credits.

On the other hand, high schools are for young adults entering the ninth, tenth, eleventh, and twelfth grades. Hopefully you will know which path you will be taking. GED and high school classes take different amounts of time to complete. GED programs for adults can take as much time as needed until requirements are met and the GED exam is passed. But high school takes a minimum of three to four years to complete.

High school for young adults depends on the kind of neighborhood they live in. Most kids attend high school in their community, but some don't because of certain circumstances. For example, I didn't attend my neighborhood high school because I made my case clear to my middle school that I wouldn't thrive or do well there. Other students might choose to go to a private school, which can be outside of their neighborhood.

There are no exact rules to doing well in your GED program or high school because most of your classes are set for you to have fun and learn to love learning about different subjects. However, to be successful in a high school or a GED program, I think you need to be prompt. This is something I learned the hard way because, as an African, I did everything in African time. If you don't know what I am talking about, this term simply means I was always late. I might not be an hour or thirty minutes late, but I was late. If you operate on African time, that needs to change. School starts early in the morning, and it's your job as a student to be there on time. Even better, try to be the first student in every class you have.

The second important thing is to ask questions when you don't understand what the teacher is talking about. Asking questions in class will help you improve your communication skills and help you get rid of nerves during class presentations. Then you have to try your very best to complete all homework assignments. If you need additional homework help, ask your teacher for assistance or to direct you to where you can get tutoring.

During this stage in your education, your homework assignments are a very good percentage of your grade while exams and quizzes are probably way less. I remember using my high school's after-school program. It was a place for me to get tutoring help. I also got to go on field trips and see my friends after school. During this time in your education, you actually have more time than you think. This means you have time for extracurricular activities, whether that's learning to play an instrument, volunteering, participating in community services, playing sports, or working. However, the main point of these activities is to learn something outside of school that you can put on your resume.

A good resume is something that's highly recommended for all college applications. It's essential to prove to a college admissions board how good of a candidate you are. A good activity or skill to pick up on is reading. I cannot tell you how reading saved me from boredom and procrastination, and opened my mind to all sorts of wonders. A lot of your education will require reading, so a love for books will save you. It will also help you become a better student. Reading improves your writing and vocabulary, which will be helpful to you as well. These are the greatest skills every student needs to be a good student. If you want to be a great student, the most important thing to know is how *you* learn.

There are many ways of learning. Some of them are reading, listening, touching, and visualizing. Figure out how you learn, because everyone learns differently. Lastly, learn how to memorize what you've read. Memorizing requires you to spend a lot of time with the material you learned from the class. Memorizing will help you do well on exams and tests. These basic skills are the building blocks you will need to be successful in higher education.

CHAPTER 3

HIGH SCHOOL STUDENTS

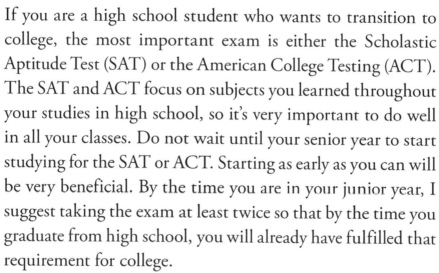

If you are a high school student who wants to transition to college, the most important exam is either the Scholastic Aptitude Test (SAT) or the American College Testing (ACT). The SAT and ACT focus on subjects you learned throughout your studies in high school, so it's very important to do well in all your classes. Do not wait until your senior year to start studying for the SAT or ACT. Starting as early as you can will be very beneficial. By the time you are in your junior year, I suggest taking the exam at least twice so that by the time you graduate from high school, you will already have fulfilled that requirement for college.

Your other focus should always be building a good resume. To do that, you must try your best to get involved in extracurricular activities throughout your high school education, as I mentioned before. Track them with this chart.

Make a list of your extracurricular activities.
1.
2.
3.
4.
5.
6.
7.

Besides having good grades, it's very important to be a well-rounded person. During your junior or senior years, most of your teachers or advisors will recommend taking honors classes or AP classes, and they will even tell you that these classes will help prepare you for college. But that is false. Your honors classes and AP classes are not like college classes. However, doing well in those classes can help you obtain college credits and save money. So study hard for your AP exams and try to score a three or better because most universities will give you credit for a three or higher, which means you won't have to take certain classes your freshman year as a college student. The most important AP classes to take are AP chemistry or biology, AP statistics or calculus, and AP literature or English.

Last but not the least, you need to have taken three or more years of a language class so you don't have to take language as a college student. I suggest learning to be fluent in at least one language so you don't have to fulfill that requirement in college. I guarantee that if you manage to score a three or better in two or more AP classes, this will exempt you from having to take an introduction level class and you will go

straight to the main or advanced classes in college. Most of these classes are three credits or more, and this is an easy way of obtaining twelve college credits minimum.

Another way to reduce your future college tuition cost is to obtain a part-time position at companies that support students. Those companies will pay a certain percentage of your tuition. Sometimes they even cover all of your tuition through tuition reimbursement. It might surprise you that most of the places you shop or grab a quick snack at like Walmart, Target, Starbucks, and Dunkin Donuts offer tuition reimbursement. Depending on which company you decide to work for, you need to work at least ten to twenty hours a week for six months to a year to receive these benefits.

At this point, it's safe to take a pause and start researching the kind of colleges you want to apply for. Track them with this chart.

Name of college	In-State or Out-of-State Tuition	GPA Requirement	SAT or ACT Requirement	How Many Letters of Recommendation Required?
1.				
2.				
3.				
4.				
5.				

The cost of your college education depends on many factors. If you choose to attend college outside of the state you live in, the expense is more. This is called out-of-state tuition. Having a GPA requirement higher or lower than what the school requires also contributes to the cost. If you have a lower GPA and SAT or ACT compared to a school's requirement, most colleges will not offer you their highest merit scholarships. But if you do get into the college that you desire with a higher GPA and SAT or ACT score, the school will give you their highest merit scholarship. If you are lucky, they will offer you a presidential scholarship, which means the school will cover your full tuition for all four years. To keep such a scholarship, you will be required to maintain a certain GPA, which varies according to the college.

If you have worked hard up to this point, earned twelve college credits minimum, and obtained a presidential scholarship, you have won the ultimate jackpot. But if you were not able to do so, there is still a chance for you to afford higher education by applying for FAFSA (Free Application for Federal Student Aid) and scholarships. FAFSA is an application to obtain government tuition assistance. You have to pay this amount back when you graduate. The application website is www.fafsa.gov.

Unlike the FAFSA, scholarships are money you earn and do not have to pay it back. Some scholarships are given annually while others are a one-time payment. Every scholarship has different requirements, and you can find websites online that explain them. You can also ask local business owners and school counselors to help you find local scholarships in the area where you live.

By the time you are a senior, you should have sent in your college applications and be awaiting your acceptances. One of the most important things to do during this period is to go on tours of your top three schools. It's important to show colleges you are interested in becoming a future student. Also, attend prospective student day at a college of your interest if you are invited. Prospective student day gives high school students a day or even two to live on campus and attend classes related to their major. This can also help you decide what school to attend when you get your acceptance letters.

So let me sum up the most important things to do as a high school student going into college.

1. Prepare for the SAT.
2. Get involved in three or more extracurricular activities.
3. Build your resume (by volunteering, shadowing, internships, etc.)
4. Take AP and honors classes.
5. Pick your top colleges.
6. Apply for scholarships and financial aid.
7. Go on college tours and prospective student days.

If you can do everything on this list, you are on a very good track to success. So now you can look forward to prom and graduation and probably catching up on sleep.

CHAPTER 4

MY HIGH SCHOOL EXPERIENCE

I decided in my last year of middle school that I wouldn't be attending the high school that most kids from my middle school transitioned to. I attended middle school at the Colfax Spanish Academy because I was labeled as a student who learned English as a second language and my school required me to take ESL class. But most of my schoolteachers didn't know that English was actually my first language. My mother made sure I learned English way before I learned my native language because deep down she knew I would always hear and learn my native tongue. She also knew that Ghana, my country of birth, was changing the education system by teaching kids English and French in school. But I was extremely shy and lacked the skills to take tests and present projects in class. Worst of all, I hated public speaking. With time I grew out of my shyness and gained those skills to better myself.

So during the eighth grade I decided I wouldn't attend Taylor Alderdice, the high school right across from my middle school. The school was way too big. I knew I would do better in a smaller school because I needed to have a professional relationship with my teachers. But I still had to find a high school to attend before the next school year. So I came home that same day and asked Google to give me a list of high schools in my area. I knew most of the schools and had attended summer camp at one before, but one school stood out: the Pittsburgh Science and Technology Academy.

At the time the high school was only three years old, but the building was once another high school called Frick High School. What stood out to me was how modern the school looked on the inside. It focused on helping students acquire STEM jobs and careers. It offered free laptops to all students to use in school and at home. It also offered a free bus pass so students living farther away could attend. Most importantly, the high school was located right in the heart of Oakland and close to the University of Pittsburgh, which was the university I had always wanted to attend.

I immediately applied. Two months into the summer, I received a letter of acceptance and attended orientation, which gave students and parents information about attending high school, including rules and policies on lateness, student duties, and the dress code, which was business casual. For the rest of the summer, which wasn't much time at this point, my mom and I shopped for clothes that were considered business casual.

On the first day of school, I was quite shocked. Everyone looked like kids going to a business meeting, but we were going to class. I had already printed out my schedule, and my first class of the day was homeroom, which only lasted fifteen minutes before my actual first class. I remember being a little late because I couldn't find the room, but I made it before the late bell. Of course, everyone looked at the students who walked in late, and I stood at the front of the room until the teacher told me to find a seat.

I was so nervous. I immediately realized that most of the kids knew each other. I tried to find my friend at the time because she had told me the very last week of the summer that she had gotten into the school as well, but I couldn't find her. So I sat at a table that needed one more person to complete it. For the rest of the first day, I simply asked people where certain rooms were and made it before the late bell.

During the first year of high school, I didn't have to put in much effort to do well. I did my homework in the after-school program, which usually ran from three to six o'clock, so by the time I got home, I had no homework to do. If I had an exam, I usually studied two days ahead of time, and I always did OK or super well. That was how I studied and made good grades, but during my junior and senior years, things changed. I got into the body and behavior (B&B) concentration, which was taught by Dr. Edwina Kinchington. She helped me in many ways by encouraging me to work harder and seek outside school opportunities for research. She is my mentor even to this day.

As seniors, students are highly encouraged to take AP classes. At the time, I didn't realize that doing well in those classes would help me get college credits and save me money. I was simply told to take advanced placement classes because it meant doing well in college classes, which was a complete lie. I also had to come up with my senior project. I decided to reach out to a previous mentor of mine, Dr. Parwani, to help me out with my research. We decided we would learn about a new biomarker called CD26 and its effects on prostate cancer. This project took me the whole year. On top of that, I was taking a lot of my hard classes, participating in clubs, and preparing to take the SAT.

My last semester was the only challenging part of my high school experience. I didn't know at the time that it was nothing compared to the amount of work I would have to put into college. I was able to get the score I needed to apply for the University of Pittsburgh, as well as four other universities I applied to at the time. Then I started applying for local and regional scholarships with the help of our school guidance counselor, Ms. Ashcom. I also applied to at least twenty scholarships online. At the time, if a student had attended school in the public system from kindergarten to the twelfth grade, there was a scholarship called the Pittsburgh Promise that gave students $10,000 maximum a year toward their college tuition. Since I had attended the public school system from second grade to the twelfth grade, I got a little less than that, but that set me up for my university education. My parents couldn't be any prouder.

I graduated high school and got accepted into the college of my choice. I later learned that attending a branched college campus was less expensive than attending a main campus. So I chose to accept the University of Pittsburgh at Greensburg because of the cost. It was also a good distance from all the comforts I was used to, such as my community, family, and friends. Now it was time for me to go college shopping.

CHAPTER 5

THE SUMMER BEFORE COLLEGE

Summer breaks can be filled with fun times with family and friends. But you must remember that this summer is going to make a very big impact on you, as you are about to enter into the life of a college student. I suggest hanging out with your family and friends while getting some rest for the first few weeks of summer. However, after those few weeks are over, it's time to start making some big decisions.

Around this time you should have gotten all of your acceptances from the universities you applied to. It's time for you to decide which institution works for you and your family. The college you decide to attend must fulfill your expectation of higher education and offer you the benefits to succeed as a student as well as be financially affordable for your family or even yourself. It's important for students to be able to afford their tuition or have a backup plan to pay for college. I say this because sometimes families can no longer send their children to school. It's important to understand this so that, if it happens to you, you can afford to continue your education.

It's also time to decide what you will be majoring in. It's up to you to decide whether you will major in something of interest or in something you are already good at. The other option is to major in something that challenges you. Most people go to college and major in subjects to please their families or even to continue the family interest in a specific field. Most students like this do not tend to enjoy their college experiences, and I certainly don't want that for you. The choice of your major must be yours alone, and it must be something you truly love and have a passion to learn.

When you decide your major, the first thing you want to do is to contact the school if you didn't state your major on your application. Once you contact the school, your advisor will be able to tell you the classes you will be taking during your first semester. One of the unpopular options for students to gain college credits even before their first semester in college is to attend community college during the summer. If you choose to do this, it's important to ask your advisor to tell you what community college classes you can take that will still count towards your major. Next, pick one or two classes and start taking them during this summer break.

Taking summer classes before starting your first semester as a college student is very beneficial. It gives you experience as a college student and offers another opportunity to earn college credit as well as save money. Most community colleges have classes that last six weeks, but I highly suggest taking classes that are twelve weeks over the summer because six weeks to complete a college course for the first time is going to be extremely painful. Twelve weeks is realistic.

The con of taking summer classes at a community college is they do not accept financial aid, so you have to pay for those classes out of pocket. On the other hand, it's beneficial because you will meet other students from whom you can learn, you can decide how you learn best, and you will also learn if you learn best by yourself or with others. You will also have your first experience of being taught by a professor instead of a teacher. Yes, there is a difference. But most importantly, you will learn that your notes are your best friend, and with time you will get better at taking notes in a way that helps you memorize and retain information.

Last but not the least, taking summer classes will give you your first experience of passing or failing a class. This is a very important lesson. If you pass the class, which means you earned a C+ or better, you will remember how you accomplished that grade and you can improve on it when you officially start your first semester in the fall. If you fail the class, which means you earned a C- or lower, it is okay because you get a chance to try again. Part of being successful in college is understanding that even if you fail a class, you have the option of doing it again and keeping the better grade. Also, remember that you cannot be successful without failure. It's simply a part of your college experience and a part of life. What you don't want to do is simply fail every class, because that's a waste of your time and money.

By the end of the summer, you should know where your interests lie and you will be able to decide on your major, if you have not decided already. What you are majoring in is one of the constant questions you will be asked during your freshman year. Choosing a major means choosing classes, and that means college credits as well as *money*, as I mentioned before. The earlier you decide what career you want to pursue and the major you need to get there the better. Some majors are easy and others are challenging, and it all depends on you to pick one and stick with it all four years.

The summer before I attended college, I remember not having any specific agenda. I volunteered for different events in my community, and then I joined my local library summer reading contest. This was something that had become a tradition for me, and this was the last year I could participate because it was only open to children and teens. I often participated in teen summer reading because it challenged me and was a way for me to do something I loved and earn prizes like books and, of course, tickets to different amusement parks in Pittsburgh.

Besides that, I mostly did what most kids in Pittsburgh do in the summer. I went to the zoo, went to church picnics, met up with friends, etc. But I did one thing I hadn't done every summer: I attended summer orientation at the university I decided to attend. Some kids and parents do not think summer orientation is necessary because they attended the prospective student day, tours, and other orientations built to help freshmen. However, I suggest that parents and students attend summer orientation. It is better to be equipped with as much knowledge as possible, especially if you are the first in your family to attend college.

Summer orientation is usually a two- or three-day event at a university or college. It involves you moving onto campus. However, parents can decide if they want to stay or leave and come back the next day. During your stay, you live with two or three roommates. This can be a good or bad thing depending on the kind of roommates you get. But most likely you will end up using your social skills to make friendships and connections. Your roommate might end up being your new best friend, study mate, lunch buddy— the list goes on. During summer orientation, you are given your class schedule and students are introduced to the main professors in each major. You'll take math and language placement exams. International students will also take the English proficiency exam.

There is time for fun too. There are a lot of events, including eating and interacting with other students through ice breakers. Students get to explore the campus and find the buildings where their classes will be held before the official first day of school. These kinds of events help students get a tiny experience of what it's going to be like as a college student.

Another thing I did the summer before my freshman year was go college shopping, so there were many trips to Kohl's, Target, Bed Bath & Beyond, etc. I recommend buying the basic items in the city where you live and buying the essentials when you get to the city or town the university is in. This helps you limit the number of vehicles that will be storing and helping you move on your move-in day.

CHAPTER 6

MOVE-IN DAY

The night before your official move-in day will be the most exciting and emotional period for most students. Usually students are leaving their cities, states, or even countries to live on campus. In the summer, you will get a notification from the university of your choice that tells you the date and time that you need to move onto campus. You probably will not realize how fast the day comes.

On move-in day, it's very important to get started early. So wake up early and get your things into a reliable vehicle. Be sure to make a list in advance and check off all the major items that you will need. You don't want to be halfway on the journey and realize you left something really important behind. Have a good breakfast before leaving and take a few snacks with you because it will be a long road trip for some of you.

Other students might be moving to a different state, so a road trip to the airport is only the beginning of their journey.

Then they will get on a plane and make another road trip to campus. A small but significant group are also coming from a different country, culture, religion, or background. They are on their way to campus for the same reason as you. I only mention this because it is important to understand that you are driving to campus alongside each other. For some, this will be the first time you are leaving home for a long period of time. You are so excited to get a taste of freedom and do things at your own liberty.

Depending on the time you arrive on campus, there might be a line before you can pull up to the designated location. Student leaders such as a CA (community assistant) and RD (residence director) will be there to welcome you and your family to campus, as well as provide you with the key to your dorm. You should be able to get to your residence because you attended summer orientation or school tour, which will give you a sense of direction in your new home.

Most freshmen are given traditional style dormitories. This means you will likely have more than one roommate. You will have bunk beds, desks, and closets that you have to share and a bathroom inside the room or a community bathroom that the whole floor shares. The good thing about community bathrooms is that campus staff clean it every day.

By the time you finally make it to your building and room, your CA or RA will have given you other information in a folder, which will contain your school ID and other information you will probably not look at. You will unload your items in the presence of your other roommates and their parents and the friends they brought with them on their journeys. This moment is important because you will make new friends very fast and become familiar with their families. For some of you there was no option to pick roommates because you didn't know anyone; you will meet your roommates and their families on the same day. This moment might get overwhelming and a bit competitive, as everyone comes to school with different things that are considered essential.

Another thing to keep in mind is that not everyone comes from the same social class. You might get a roommate that has everything and another that has almost nothing. After you get settled in and everyone's parents leave, you will be left with just your roommates. Usually there is a lot of crying and praying; it gets emotional when your loved ones leave you. But I promise you that, with time, you will determine a good balance with your family and friends.

After your parents leave, you will continue setting up your room. One of the most important stations in the room to set up is your bed. After a long road trip and day with your family and new roommates, you are going to be so tired. Set up your bed up first so you don't have to do it later. The second most important place is your desk. Now, everyone is different in how they set up this area, but everyone's desk is a reflection of his or her personality. It's also a display of what's important to you. Every student has a different desk setup. I suggest placing few personal books that you are reading for fun or any items that represent your faith like the Bible or the Koran on your desk. Next, I recommend at least one thing to place on the wall above your desk, such as a poster with your favorite motivational quote. Third, you want to put a picture of something from home like a picture of your family, pet, best friend, or significant other. Make sure whatever picture you choose makes you feel happy.

Next comes your closet space or just any space in general that you want to set up with your clothes and shoes. If you are in a traditional dorm where the ratio of closets to roommates is low, it's important to have a talk and decide how much room in the closets each roommate can have. Besides the closet, there are other places to store your items, such as under your bunk bed. After hanging up your clothing for the season, it's important to store other clothes for different seasons in bins or suitcases under your bunk bed. This way the room remains spacious and your clothing and shoes are in a safe place.

Sometimes move-in days can be overwhelming. But it's important to be well-equipped in order to have a successful day. Before going to bed, make sure to pick out your first outfit and put your school supplies in your backpack. Last but not the least, go to sleep early so you can wake up on time and get ready for your very first day of college. Move-in day can be extremely exhausting, but that's no excuse to miss your first class or even breakfast on your first day of class.

CHAPTER 7

FRESHMAN YEAR, FIRST SEMESTER

The basic building blocks of being a freshman in your first semester are very simple. I think consistency is key to having a successful semester and, of course, freshman year. The most common question asked you will be asked in your freshman year, especially in your first semester, is what your major is. Most ice breakers in your classes will begin with your name, where you are from, and why you choose the college or university you are attending.

The following are a couple of the most frequently asked questions by freshmen in their first semester and my answers.

1. How do I choose the right major?

After every student has announced his or her major in every class during your first day of school, you will realize right away with whom you have a common interest and who you do not. Your advisors will also ask your major during your first one-on-one meeting with them. As I have mentioned, before it's important to know what your interests are and what major you are pursuing because you save time and money. But if you haven't decided yet, it's really important to know that there is still time. You can choose to be undecided for now or you can make your own major. Making your own major is new in some institutions, but it is an option. If you choose to take that path, you will need the help of your advisor to find a new advisor who knows more about the classes you need to take to get that degree.

For those of you who have decided your major, it's important to make sure you are under an advisor who has good knowledge about the classes you need to take to get your degree. If at any point you feel misled by your advisor, you can ask for a new one. Sometimes students feel that it hurts the advisor's feelings or they want to avoid confrontation with their advisors. But it's simply a waste of your time and money to stay with a bad advisor, take all these classes, and find out at the end of your college experience that you can't graduate because you are missing credits and have to take two or three more classes to finish your degree. I have seen this happen to students time after time. Trust me. You don't want to be in that position.

2. I was a straight-A student in high school and I expect to get straight As as a freshman in college. How do I get straight As?

As a freshman, one of the classes you have to take is called freshman seminar. One of the activities of this class is to predict how your semester is going to go based on observation. One of the things that you will be asked is based on your grades for the classes you are taking. You can believe me when I say that as long as you attend class and do not miss any days, you will get an A in the freshman seminar. But that might not be the case for every class.

Overall, it's good to have expectations and work hard toward your goals, but at the same time, it's good to be realistic and have faith in yourself because sometimes things do work out. The sad truth is that most freshmen are not able to get straight As their first semester because the level of hard work it takes is different compared to what they are used to in high school. Most students do very badly because they misjudge the level of effort and work they have to put into their classes to do well. But something is for sure: no matter what your final grades are after your first semester, you can only get better.

3. Does attendance matter?

It depends on the class. Sometimes a professor will tell you that attendance is not required and all you need to do is pass your exams. Other professors will say there will be unexpected quizzes and lots of class discussions so class attendance is required. Some professors require attendance because attendance is a percentage of your final grade. Attendance both can and cannot be a requirement because it all depends on your professor and the agenda of the class.

4. How can I pay for all my books? They are so expensive!

My simple answer to this question is to simply *rent*, not buy, books. My freshman year, I remember spending so much money on books. I was also worried about where I was going to store them when I got back home. But after my first semester, things changed. I made friends who introduced me to book rental services. I highly recommend Chegg because students can send their books back in the same box they came in at the end of the semester. The best part is that Chegg provides you with a shipping label to ship the books back for *free*. There are other websites like Amazon that provide similar services. You just have to use your resources to find them.

5. How can I get extra help in my classwork and homework if I am struggling in a class?

You might not be in the position to get help at the beginning of the semester because you might not be struggling in any of your classes at the moment. After some homework, quizzes, and maybe the failure of your first exam, you may want to seek help in one or two of your classes. The best way to seek help is to find one-on-one tutoring from a student who has taken the class you are in. I suggest going to the tutoring center at your college and university and filling out forms to request tutoring. If all tutors are occupied, you can seek other options of tutoring through Chegg tutoring. The service costs $14.95 to subscribe to get homework help. Besides that, you can always ask to go to your professor's office hours and ask about homework help.

6. I miss my family. So can I go home every weekend?

After a few months of staying on campus, you might be surprised when you start to feel homesick. If you have a vehicle, you might think of going home over the weekends. But I highly suggest that you resist the temptation. I can start by telling you all the reasons it's a bad idea. If you go home or continue to go home, you will never be independent and you will never grow as an individual from your family. Also, you will not learn a few adult things that you need to learn to grow from being a teenager to an adult. You will also miss out on making stronger connections with your peers. Lastly, going home might be a big distraction and you might get behind on doing your homework or studying for exams. It's important and even beneficial to go home during holiday breaks, but you should stay on campus throughout the academic school year.

7. What do I do if I don't get along with my roommates?

Hopefully you are never in a situation where you are among roommates that do not like themselves or do not like you. If you don't pick specific people to become your roommates, most universities will give you a questionnaire to decide what kind of roommates to give to you. Depending on whether you picked your best friends or got to have roommates that are total strangers, situations do occur in which you and your roommates might not get along. If you ever can't get along with your roommates for a long period, there is more than one way to solve this problem.

The first thing to do is to have a roommate meeting where everyone is present so you and your roommates can talk about the problem and come to a resolution. If that does not work well or if a roommate does not attend the meeting, the next plan of action is to ask your CA to set a roommate meeting. Usually in situations like this there is a need to inform and involve an authoritarian figure who can come into the situation and address the issue quickly. If things continue to stay the same or if things get worse with your roommate situation, it's best to ask for a room or dorm change. This might require you to fill out some papers and have a meeting with the RD or student housing director. Then you'll have to move all your stuff to a new dorm. Don't feel bad for deciding to make a room change. Depending on the situation, it can do you good to move away from such circumstances.

8. What is a meal plan or flex? Which one should I choose?

Disclaimer: Flex might be called something different depending on the university or college you attend.

Meal plans or flex do the same thing in that they simply allow you to purchase food in the school store or cafeteria. A meal plan allows you to get food in the cafeteria once or twice a day. Flex allows you to buy snacks at the school snack store or cafeteria. If you are a student who lives on campus, it's recommended that you get the meal plan with flex. But if you are a student who lives at home, you might just need to get flex so you can buy a meal or a snack between classes.

Additional tips

Of course, there are more questions that students have about life on campus. However, the ones covered in this chapter are a few that I can recall were important to me. During this period, it's important to ask questions when you do not have an answer or a solution to something. I will start with your dorm and the residence where you live. It's important to know that when you have a problem in your room, such as a broken toilet, you need to fill out a form and then notify your CA. If you have problems with your roommates, you can inform your CA or RD. The next most important thing is your classes and your professors. It's important to figure out with your advisor how many classes you need to take to graduate and what your plan B will be if you fail a class. It's important to find good seating in your classes so you can see the professor and the overhead or class board.

Sometimes, depending on what you are learning, you need to decide how you will be taking your class notes. You may not take notes the same way, depending on the class. I strongly recommend note-taking with by hand before or after class. If you are too shy to ask questions in class, stay after to ask the professor questions. You can also attend office hours if you have longer questions. In any class, the most important document given to students is the syllabus, and it will be useful throughout the semester. Besides your textbooks, the syllabus is considered every college student's holy bible. The syllabus will tell you which chapters you will need to read in your books. Some syllabus shows the daily agenda of what you will be doing for the entire semester. I highly suggest utilizing your syllabus for chapter readings, quizzes, and exam updates. It's key to look at your syllabus before going to class.

If you are a student with a disability, it's important to make that known to your professors so they can show you the best way to get the proper resources and guidance to help you be successful in class. I highly encourage you to ask all questions, even the ones you think are irrelevant and unimportant. Sometimes students believe their questions are stupid, but what they don't know is that other students who are equally afraid might have the same questions. The stupidest question is the one that has not been asked, and I learned this the hard way. If you happen to have questions and do not want to ask in class, there are other options. One is to wait before and after class to ask your professor questions. Another is to attend your professor's office hours. Throughout the school year, I can tell you that attending my professors' office hours was the best method for me to learn what was going on in the class. It is also a great way to build a relationship with your professors, which will be beneficial when you ask them for a letter of recommendation.

Now let's talk your personal or social life as a student. It's important to have a balance so that you can be successful in all areas of your life. It's important to talk to your family regularly, not just on days when you performed badly on an exam or had an argument with your roommates or boyfriend. As a student living on campus, you need to establish a time and frequency for talking with your family. It's also important to establish when they can come to visit you and when you can go home to visit them. I also highly suggest getting to know as many people as possible in your area of interest. That could include students in your major and students in clubs you are hopefully a member of. Being part of clubs will increase your social circle. Having a good social circle can either make you a better student or a bad student. If you can find a group of friends that you can go out and have fun with and study with and form study groups with, you have won the jackpot.

Another important aspect of being a first-year student in your first semester is the experience of being broke. Yes, being broke is a part of the college or university experience. It will seem like no matter how much you get in allowance from your parents or paycheck, there will be times when you are broke. Because you are broke, you might consider getting a job if you do not have one already. If you do decide to work, I suggest applying for a work-study job. A work-study job is any position created by the university or college. Students are only allowed to work 10 hours every week, so it will not take too much of your studying time, and your work schedule will be based on your academic schedule. Now, I say this because depending on your major, it may not be beneficial to work. After all, those hours you are working are hours you could be studying and focusing. Other students might have majors that give them a lot more liberty to either work at a work-study position or a regular job. I leave it up to you to decide whether to get a job or not. At the end of the day, you as the student have to determine what is of greater value to you.

CHAPTER 8

FRESHMAN YEAR, SECOND SEMESTER

Boy, you needed that one or two days off to transition from the first semester to the second semester because you were so tired. By now you have had many experiences, such as being late for a class, missing out on an assignment, but hopefully not missing an entire exam. You have returned your old textbooks and have new ones because you have new classes, but you might be repeating one or even two classes because you underestimated the amount of work needed to be successful in college. Despite the mistakes and failures, one thing you have accomplished is finishing your first semester in college. This difficult task that many people have not accomplished, so it's important to lift your head and get ready, because although you started on the wrong foot, you want to end the school year feeling like you are on your way to landing on the right foot. So let's begin!

When you come back to campus, one of the first things you will notice is the fact that some of your peers did not come back. Besides struggling to be the best students they can be, life has a way of bringing other challenges. Sometimes this will mean your roommate, study partner, or friend left school. This might affect your emotions, but one thing you need to learn as a student in your second semester is that sometimes you have to stand alone. So now you know you didn't need your roommate for comfort and companionship or your friend to be your study partner. You might even discover that your boyfriend or girlfriend has changed from the person they used to be.

Now you need to concentrate on the new classes you have and the new professors you need to get to know to be successful in your last term of the academic year. At the same time, you might have personal struggles that you cannot equally ignore, such as your significant other, your family, or health issues. This is the time to reflect on how you studied last semester and figure how you can improve on it. There are many ways to study, and you might have realized that you can't use the same method to study for all of your classes. Some classes require a different technique to give you a full understanding of each chapter or topic discussed by the professor. Most importantly, you need to figure out what kind of a student you are and how best you understand and retain information. Take the time to investigate these things about yourself.

Another thing you need to find out about yourself is where you study best. This is different for everybody. Depending on if they are an introvert or extrovert, some people might study and concentrate better at the library or the study room in their hall. Wherever you study best, please simply find it. One place most students do not study is in the classroom. As a student, I noticed that most students came to class, sometimes on time and other times a few minutes late. However, they simply took notes from the professors' lectures and then simply left. Most students never went back to that classroom until the next session. However, one of the best methods of memorization is repetition of the same method. This means studying in the same room or even the same chair you learn from in each class. Some students could do so much better if they studied in the same room and even the same seat in which they will be taking their exams. Besides that, the lecture rooms are so large, you can spread your notes out and even use the dry erase markers and board to solve problems in a bigger space. This method helped me in my math classes and upper biology courses when I needed to work on every problem and understand each step in the problem. Stay in those classrooms and study as long as you want. Even if you stay there until the building closes for the day, it will pay off.

In this period in your academic career, it's also important to get to know who is who on your campus. It's important to know at least one of the campus police officers, a librarian, a counselor, a nurse or doctor, the presidents of certain clubs, or a professor. You want to build connections with everyone. It's also important to get your name out there. Sometimes opportunities might show up that are not yet disclosed to students. Having these connections can help get you recommended for a research position or leadership role. Having connections will take you a long way, and hopefully by now you have a group of friends you can go out and have fun with and another group of students you can study and be serious with. It is key in college to realize the kind of groups or friends you have. In my experience, I haven't seen a group of friends who can balance schoolwork, getting physically active, and having fun together effectively. There are always going to be different groups of people you enjoy those certain moments with.

If you have been unsuccessful so far in finding friends and engaging on campus, I highly suggest joining a school club. There are so many clubs on your campus, and you have probably already attended a couple campus events held by student clubs. School clubs can be academically based, such as clubs that are focused on different majors. Other clubs can be a way for students to participate in community service. There are also just fun clubs where students can play sports and games. Whichever club you want to join, just make sure the leadership feels right. In my experience, sometimes the club sounds wonderful but as soon as you become a member you notice the disconnect between the leaders or even the advisor of the club.

Make sure the people in the club are your kind of people, too, because you will be spending a lot of time with them one way or another. You will see them in club meetings, at club events, on campus and off, in some of your classes, at your dorm—the list goes on. If you dislike the members in your club, keep in mind that you have to see them everywhere, so make sure your personality is accepted and you are given a warm welcome before becoming an official member. Also, make sure the club meetings match with your availability.

You don't want to be a member of a club and not be able to show up to club meetings because you have class or other obligations.

So let me give you the rundown of every club on your campus. There is always a minimum of one or two advisors. The advisors oversee everything that goes on in the club, and every activity has to be approved by them. The advisor approves events based on the motto of the club. The motto is a club's purpose or main objective. The motto is different in every club, but it represents the strong principles that the club stands for and upholds at all times. The advisors of the club can be professors or any other staff of the university. The student leaders of the club usually include a president, vice president, secretary, treasurer, and sometimes a social media or newspaper informant or representative. These student leaders are elected to their positions by the members of the club on an annual basis. Also, any of those positions can be revoked if a majority of the students in the club feel like the student leader is not doing his or her job well.

So why am I telling you all of this? You are probably guessing right: I highly suggest that you become a student leader. I was a student leader and served in positions such as secretary, treasurer, and vice president. I recommend becoming a student leader as early as you can because if you wait too long it might be too late. Waiting until your junior year to become a student leader for the first time might be harder because most club members want to be familiar with their leaders. The second semester of your freshman year is the perfect time to become a member of a club and start looking at the kind of student leadership positions your academic schedule and social schedule will allow. Becoming a student leader also makes you important in the eyes of the university and the staff. Most people will know your name based on your position. Student leaders are treated well by the university, and everyone holds you to a higher standard in every aspect of your student life.

Every club on campus is recognized during a leadership conference or ceremony, and certain clubs are given awards in different categories, such as raising the most money for charity or the best club. These awards are earned because the student body votes for clubs to get those awards. From my experience, there is no greater feeling than when clubs and club members get on stage to receive an award and everyone is smiling for the camera because you might be seen on the local news or campus news or in the newspaper. I don't know any parents who don't like to see their kids being highlighted in the media for doing good things.

Now, if you decide to remain a regular member of the club, it's very important to contribute to the club as much as you can. You can do this by voicing your opinion and giving your suggestions when student leaders talk about the kind of projects and community events they want to be involved in next semester or next school year. Offering to help the club set up tables and chairs during events or taking charge of an event are also ways regular members can add to the value of the club. This is a way you can show other students and the student leaders that you can handle things and take charge. That will help you become a student leader in that club.

Last but not least, I suggest you join a club that pertains to your major. Most of the time the advisors in the major clubs are the heads of those majors' departments. It's good to become a club member early so the advisors know you and you can develop a relationship with them over the years, which will help you get mentors, shadowing opportunities, and letters of recommendation.

As you get to the end of the semester, I think it's important to realize how far you have come. Even if your goal to get straight As didn't work out, it's important to realize that you can retake classes in which you want to improve your grade. If you came into the academic school year as an undecided major, I hope by now you have decided with the help of the internet, your advisor, and career services programs. Remember to keep working hard. As the season changes and it gets warmer, sometimes students lose their focus and want to hang out with their friends instead of focusing on their schoolwork and academics.

You might notice during this time that most people do not care. If your professors were taking attendance, they probably stopped doing that. If there were forty students in your class, now there might be ten. Out of the ten, maybe six are always ten minutes late for a lecture. But there is that one student who's always the last person to leave class and the first to get to class. You want that student to be you.

As you are about to finish up finals week, you want to do two things: First, mark down in your agenda book the time, place, and day of each final exam. If you have more than two exams on a single day, you can always ask your professor to take it on a different day and usually they will work with you on that. Second, schedule your summer classes. This is where you probably are rolling your eyes at me and saying "But … but what about my family vacation, and what if I want to work and get some money for the next school year?" Trust me. I know how hard this will be, but at the end of the day, this sacrifice will pay off. That I can promise you.

CHAPTER 9

THE SUMMER BEFORE
YOUR SOPHOMORE YEAR

This is your first summer back home, and I know you miss your dog or cat, mom and dad, and maybe your siblings, but I will keep your secret. All your mind and body are telling you is that you need sleep, time with your family, and enjoyment of summer sports or even travel. Well, guess what. You can still do those things and get some college credits. It's important that at the very beginning of summer break you take your time to do what you please in moderation because you have two weeks or less before summer classes start.

Make a couple of calls starting with your advisor and ask him or her what kind of summer classes are offered in your major that the university you attend. He or she will probably take the time to break down the classes that are electives and the ones that pertain to your major that you can take either on campus or on another campus. Now you are probably asking yourself which of the available classes you want to take based on the professors teaching those classes. It might be a small or large pool. My simple answer is you should take the advanced level classes pertaining to your major. It's good to challenge yourself because sometimes you have to train your mind to be able to learn things quickly. On the other hand, you can take the easy electives such as writing, English comprehension, or art and music to get those out of the way so you can focus on taking the classes that are most important to your major during the school year.

Going back to school at the university you attend might be a far commute for you if you live in a different state or country. If that's your situation, you'll want to ask your advisor if there are any community colleges or local universities where you live which they will accept college credits and for what classes. The next thing to do is register and find out how much those classes cost, classes' start and end dates, as well as your new professor's information. Basically the same thing you did at the beginning of your first and second semesters.

Disclaimer: summer classes are not easy. They are mostly six- or twelve-week courses. The summer semester is broken up into two semesters, the first and second six or twelve weeks. With that in mind, I want you to be alert in your studies. Make sure you show up on time and do what you have been doing during the normal school year. The advantage of taking summer classes is that you get ahead in earning good grades and college credits toward your degree. The classes are usually smaller because not everyone is taking the opportunity to get ahead. You will probably build a better relationship with your professors and get to know them better. The professors' office hours are probably longer, which gives you the opportunity to ask all the questions you desire and seek clarity. One disadvantage of summer courses is there is *no financial aid*, as I mentioned previously. That means you will not receive FAFSA if you do during the normal school year. However, there might be scholarships you can apply for through your university to help you pay for your summer tuition. Hopefully at this point you have figured out your new surroundings if you are taking summer courses at a different college or university than you attend during the school year.

Now you are probably wondering how you can go on vacation, work, and possibly hang out with your friends. The key to having both a social life and an academic life is to plan ahead. If you and your family plan on going on a staycation or vacation, make sure you know ahead of time so you can discuss missing work, tests, or quizzes with your professor. Professors prefer to know such information weeks ahead of time because it shows you care about the class and want to do well. Some professors will let you go on vacation and you can make up work when you return. Others might give you an excuse so the missing work is not included in your overall grade. Every professor is different. That's why it's key to have a professional relationship with them. It can be helpful during times like this.

I also suggest hanging out with your friends on weekend when you are probably done taking a test. There will be work during this period. Overall, to be a successful st it's good to have a balance between your academic a life. If you're like me, it was instilled in you by y stay locked up in your room and just study, ' parents don't know is that the brain and body don't work like that. Your brain is active and can retain information thirty minutes at a time. That's why you study and then take a break to do something else like going on a walk, eating a snack, or watching a YouTube video. It gives your brain a rest.

During your summer classes, try to sleep as much as you can because sleep is important to your motivation and focus. Remember to prioritize your time so that you get a good night's rest. If you are still interested in working and getting money to go back-to-school shopping, it's also a good idea. During the summertime a lot of companies are hiring, and you will probably not find it hard to get a job that's flexible in terms of scheduling for students.

If you follow these guidelines, you can finish the summer semester with six to twelve credits if you took two six-week classes or thirteen credits if you have a class with a lab. If you complete twelve or thirteen credits, that's a whole semester completed. This means instead of attending four years of college, you will attend college for three and a half years. If you attended a community college, this also means you saved lots of money.

After your last six weeks in the summer term, you might have a few weeks left before going back to campus. Make sure to start packing your things again and do additional shopping for the new school year. For those of you who stayed on campus and attended summer school at your actual university college, you are probably packing up your things just to back in a few weeks for the normal school year. During weeks you have left in summer break, spend your In the eyes of your parents, you are growing up so quickly and you are so independent now and they probably don't want to say it but they've missed you with all the time you have been spending on your academics, work, and friends.

Also, remember to check your school's website for the classes you want and need to take next semester. If you have any questions, make sure to email or call your advisor for help. Remember that your class schedule isn't set in stone; it can change to accommodate your preferences, especially in those elective classes. Also, you may not be required to stay in the freshman traditional dorm anymore. You may be able to apply to have different housing with your friends, which is always exciting because you can choose to live in an apartment-style dorm with your buddies. Life is simply getting easier, and you are getting smarter in every aspect.

CHAPTER 10

SOPHOMORE YEAR, FIRST SEMESTER

———◦———

You are probably on that same road trip you took a year ago to the same destination. Others might also be on the same path to the same destination. That's because school is back in session! You have completed your first year in college and your first summer semester. At this point, you probably have a minimum of thirty college credits completed or thirty-six to thirty-seven if you took summer classes. That is a huge accomplishment, and now you are back in the regular academic school year for your sophomore year.

During this time you might notice some new and old faces. Some of those new faces are freshmen students, and they probably remind you of yourself a year ago when you were in their position. Some of those new students are transfer students from a different college or university who might be in the same academic year as you. By this point you are probably familiar with the buildings on your campus, so there is no need to go on a mini scavenger hunt to find where exactly your classes will be held. You have enough knowledge now that you can find your classes on your first day of class. You have probably moved into your new dorm and have been catching up with your buddies on their summer experiences and getting to know their families during move-in day. This is a good time to print out the syllabus for each class and start organizing your space again for the new school year. You might also realize through conversations with others that some people in your year and major have either dropped out or transferred to a different university. This will be constant throughout your academic experience.

By your sophomore year, you have passed the basic and general classes and are now about to take some advanced courses that pertain to your major. Your professors have higher expectations of you and they expect you to memorize and retain information from past classes and apply it to the new knowledge you will be learning. They expect your papers to have little to no grammar or spelling errors. There is no excuse for late work or missed assignments without prior notice. Your professors also expect you to know the proper resources on campus if you need tutoring, IT help, etc., for the course. Your test or quizzes might be longer and you will have access to inside and outside information on most topics taught by your professor.

At the same time, your social circle is expanding and so are your extracurricular activities. If you were in a club your freshman year, you will be having a new club election. This is your chance to become a student leader and prove to not just the other members of the club but to yourself that you can be a leader. It's important to have friendly competition and campaign if you are applying for a high position in the club such as president or vice president. If at any time you realize the campaign is hostile, I suggest leaving the position and letting the proper authorities know. That could be the advisors of the club or the person in charge of student activities at the university or college you attend.

By now you are probably better at managing your time, so if you are looking to get a job to make a little money, this is the time to do so. Working ten hours a week as a college student has little to no impact on a student's academics. Depending on your major, you might be able to work more than ten hours a week or exactly ten hours. Each semester there are job postings on your university or college website where you can start your job hunt. Most of these positions allow students to only work ten hours a week and are mostly flexible jobs. If you do not find a job on campus, I suggest looking for flexible jobs off campus. It's important to find a job that understands your obligation as a student and that will have someone ready to work your shift in case you don't feel well that day or you unexpectedly have three exams that week and need to focus on your academics.

At this point, I think it's safe to say you are a student who wants to succeed and it's up to you to decide what is a major priority to you and what is not. Life is what you make it. Sometimes others might have to work less because of their God-given talents or their family's educational background. You might have to work harder to keep up with someone from such a background because you might be an ESL student or the first person in your family to go to college. The grind is harder, but you will have a greater victory for yourself and your family in the end.

Maintaining an underdog mindset will make it easier to wake up early to go to classes or work. When someone asked me in college how I could wake up at five in the morning on a weekday to study and go to work, I simply laughed. They didn't know I was the first person in my immediate family to go to college in the US. I had a lot to lose or gain depending on what I made my priority. I knew of many students of African heritage who went to college and came back home as a dropout, pregnant, or addicted to drugs or substances. Knowing that, I was very careful in the kind of friends I made and I was motivated at all times. It didn't matter if I was up doing schoolwork at three in the morning and I had to wake up at eight to get to class. I kept thinking about what a privilege it was for me to get the chance to have a higher education. This appreciation grew as I saw more and more of my classmates leave because of financial difficulty.

One thing is for sure your sophomore year: the struggle is very real. But keeping all my tips and tricks in mind and maintaining a disciplined lifestyle will surely pay off throughout the entire school year.

CHAPTER 11

THE NEXT TWO YEARS

It might be hard for you to imagine what your sophomore and junior years will look like. However, the next two years will look like what you make them look like and how hard you work for it. You must set goals every single day and make it your business and priority to achieve those goals. Being a student does not exempt you from the troubles and struggles of life. Most students struggle in their relationships, health, academics, and spirituality. Others struggle with simple things like making friends. I had a professor who started class every week by asking students where they stand in their academics, self-care, family, and spirituality to remind them to maintain a balance in all aspects of their lives.

Start each day by doing the simple things and work your way to the hardest things if that's how you operate. Other students like me like to do the difficult things first and work up to the easy stuff. You might also notice that most students are in relationships and you might not be. That is okay. A lot of people think one of the benefits of college is meeting their life partners. That happens for some people, but it doesn't work for others. It's hard to understand why everyone seems happy and in a relationship when you are single and unhappy. The truth is that most students do not maintain their relationships all four years. Keep in mind that there are plenty of people in your shoes and if you don't meet your significant other in college, you will meet them somewhere else. As you grow in your academics and advance to higher stages, a romantic relationship might not be something you think or worry about.

When you are about to enter your junior year, one of the major questions students are asked by their professors has to deal with their senior project. Depending on your major, you might already have an idea of what kind of question or focus you want to research for your senior project. You can decide what kind of senior project you want to conduct by looking at the posters of last year's projects around the department building of your school. Looking at previous experiments or research can help you decide what kinds of research has already been done, which can help you form a new idea. You can even try a different approach or method to answer a question someone has already tried to answer.

One thing you need to remember when it comes to your senior project is that you have a lot of freedom to choose what kind of project you want to work on. Do not allow people to limit your ideas and methods. You have an option to work on a group project or independently. If you choose to work in a group, it's important to make sure everyone is on board and has a way to contact one another. You need a group in which every individual is assigned a part so that in the end the project will be completed. Your senior project is very important because the outcome will decide if you graduate or not. This is the last important requirement before you get your degree, so it's important to put all your energy into this while at the same time doing well and passing your other classes.

Sometimes students get senioritis. I have seen it firsthand. Some of the most serious students relax. While this might work for some, it doesn't work out for everyone and can lead to disappointment and regret. During this time, I think it's important to have fun, decorate your cap and gown, and even plan your graduation party. But when it's time to get your schoolwork done, it's important to maintain the same amount of excitement. For some of you, this might be the last year you are in school because you have accomplished all your academic goals. So it's a bigger celebration. For some students, this degree is only a ticket to further your education or a stepping-stone to get your foot into the right career. This is why senior year is so important for students who are looking to further their education.

CHAPTER 12

YEAR FOUR

Four years go by fast, but for some people, time flies when personal things, health, and relationships play a role in getting your degree. Your senior year can be totally different than any year yet. By now you have been a college student for three or four years and should have a lot of confidence in your abilities as a student. You also have a system that works for you. You can balance school, your social life, your spiritual life, as well as your family and friends. You have stayed up and survived standardized testing and completing so much of the requirements for your degree.

If you have followed my plan from the beginning, you might already be done and on your way to being a degree holder. That's the goal, for you to finish your college experience spending the least amount of money and wasting the least amount of time. However, if you are still going through your fourth or even fifth year, that is okay too. Realistically, some students will end up going to college for four or more years.

A lot of things happen in three to four years. It's also a short period when it comes to academia.

These are some of the reasons someone might go to college or university for more than four years:

1. A student took a break for a semester or year.
2. A student lost a family member.
3. A student got married.
4. A student lost their financial sponsor.
5. A student realized that college was not for them and changed their mind.
6. A student is pursuing more than one degree.

Whatever the reason, every student is different and you are probably in one of those six situations if you have been going to college for four years or more. My best advice for super seniors, which is anyone who has been in college for more than four years, is to keep working hard because being a college or university student is *not* a permanent position. Read that again. Sometimes it might feel like you will never graduate and will be a student forever, but this is not true. Whatever your goals for graduation are, that should be your main focus. Everyone has a different goal. Some people even want to go further and get a master's degree or PhD. Remember that those who wait patiently are usually the ones who get the last laugh.

For those of you who want to go to graduate school, remember that Cs get degrees but A and Bs will increase your chances of getting into grad school and PhD programs. Grades only make up a percentage of the qualifications graduate and doctorate schools are looking for. Your personal statement, letter of recommendation, GRE or other test scores, resume, and interview make up a bigger percentage. So do not worry too much about grades because in the end more than one of the requirements will be in your favor.

As a senior hoping to pursue a graduate or doctorate degree after completing your undergraduate studies, it's essential to do your research. You need to research schools and the requirements needed to apply to them just like you did four years ago when you were a high school student applying for colleges. You need to attend school tours and orientations to show your interest in the institution and program. This might be overwhelming. It's important that if at any point this process truly becomes too much for you, you should take a break. You can still apply for programs to graduate schools and PhD programs after graduation.

CHAPTER 13

GRADUATION

Everything you have worked for over the past three, four, or even five years has led you to this moment. Your graduation day! Your graduation will be filled with lots of tears, laughter, and joy because this is the moment you will embrace all your hard work. It is also a time when your parents and loved ones can stand proud and say how their hard work to put you through school has come to a happy ending.

Getting ready for graduation might be stressful because you are balancing a bit of schoolwork while thinking about one of the most exciting moments in your life. By all means, the first thing you have to do is to apply for graduation. In most cases, applying for graduation can occur at the beginning of the first semester or second semester of your senior year. Applying for graduation requires you to have twelve credits or less to complete your degree. After applying for graduation, you need to complete the rest of the credits to fully complete the program. Then your advisor, as well as staff members of your university, will start informing you about dates for graduation, how many people each student is allowed to invite, and the cost of the graduation gown and cap. These conversations and purchases should make it easier to start preparing for your day.

Start by making a list of people you want to invite based on the amount of people the university allows each student to have. Depending on the size of the university or college you attend, this might be a small or large number. Include important friends, family members, and other loved ones you want to share your moment with. Send the invitations that your university or college will provide you with. They usually include the location, date, and time of the ceremony.

Next, you must figure out what to wear on this day and, for us ladies, how you will do your makeup and hair. Afterward, you should start decorating your cap. I think it's always interesting to see what kind of quotes and sayings people have on their graduation caps. The most important decision on your graduation day is also after the ceremony. Some students might choose to go out with their families or have a graduation party. Graduation parties can take a lot of work and planning, so it's best to have a family member or friends help you with that. For international students, it's important to inform your loved ones ahead of time so that they can purchase plane tickets and reserve hotel as well as attend graduation parties. After graduation, it's important to go back to your dorm to make sure everything you own is packed and you get to say your final goodbyes to roommates and classmates.

During this period, students need to think about the future. That might include getting a job or furthering their education. I think it's important for all students to make these decisions ahead of time. It is even more important to embrace the moment. Some of you are the first in your family to go to college and graduate. For others, this is your last education stop. You might have other dreams and ambitions, such as getting your dream job and working your way up to your American dream. You should be very proud that you met your goal to go to college and finish successfully. Students who are minorities or come from low-income households, as well as immigrants like me, have a lesser chance of success. These groups are less informed and are not given an equal opportunity, so it is always a *great* achievement when students from these backgrounds succeed and graduate. It truly shows that anything is achievable with hard work and dedication.

CHAPTER 14

THE END OF YOUR JOURNEY WITH ME

The end of our journey is fast approaching. As you read the last few words of this book, my purpose is complete. You have been given the basic knowledge you need to be successful in college. My biggest wish is that this book will reach many women and men who are uninformed about the journey they are about to take as they start thinking about college and applying to institutions of higher education. I want to encourage immigrant students and families to realize what it takes to be a college graduate so they can start early in preparing to help their children achieve that goal. My goal is to encourage you and strengthen you because the road to success is sometimes lonely. Not many people can obtain success in higher education because most graduates do not talk about it or help others. This was the purpose of writing this book. To give back to students and families if you have any questions or need one-on-one coaching I can be reached at <u>doyouwanttogotocollegenow@</u> <u>gmail.com</u>.

ACKNOWLEDGMENTS

I want to first thank the Almighty God for giving me the knowledge and bravery to write this book from my experience. Next I want to thank my family and friends for their constant support and encouragement. I also want to thank my teachers and mentors, who have largely contributed to the intellectual women I am today, for encouraging me to always be curious and think outside the box in my studies.

Printed in the United States
by Baker & Taylor Publisher Services